For Your Garden

GARDEN ACCENTS

For Your Garden

GARDEN ACCENTS

WARREN SCHULTZ

FRIEDMAN/FAIRFAX
P U B L I S H E R S

A FRIEDMAN/FAIRFAX BOOK

© 1996 by Michael Friedman Publishing Group, Inc.

Library of Congress Cataloging-in-Publication Data available upon request.

ISBN 1-56799-265-X

Editor: Susan Lauzau
Art Directors: Jeff Batzli and Lynne Yeamans
Photography Editor: Colleen Branigan
Production Associate: Camille Lee

Color separations by Fine Arts Repro House Co., Ltd.
Printed in China by Leefung-Asco Printers Ltd.

For bulk purchases and special sales, please contact:
Friedman/Fairfax Publishers
Attention: Sales Department
15 West 26th Street
New York, New York 10010
212/685-6610   FAX 212/685-1307

Table of Contents

INTRODUCTION

*F*rom *their very beginnings as the pleasure grounds of the ancient Near East, gardens have been artful combinations of living plants and man-made ornaments. Gardens are where human nature and mother nature exist in harmony.*

As earthbound representations of paradise, gardens have been adorned through the ages with statues of deities and spirits. Over time, garden accents became more earthly and practical, though no less artful. From the magnificent fountains of Persia to the elaborate steps of Italian Renaissance gardens to the cast-iron benches of Victorian England, garden ornaments reflect the times.

A more democratic garden tradition is based on utility. While the gardens of the nobility were decorative testaments to the timelessness of beauty, the early gardens of all but the upper classes were based on the no-nonsense need to raise food. But before long, ornamental gardening expanded its provenance.

Until recently, conformity was the rule in most gardens. Foundation plantings and wide expanses of lawn, shoulder to shoulder with neighboring yards, left little room for personal accents.

Fortunately, all that is changing. A new, eclectic garden style has emerged, allowing for individual expression through design, plantings, and ornaments. The landscape becomes a melting pot of gardening styles, ranging from Florentine urns to rustic wagon wheels to glass gazing balls.

Nature supplies the living, growing heart of the garden. We can only arrange nature's artwork to suit our tastes. But we can add a personal stamp with our choice of ornaments in the garden. These accents provide a window into the soul of the gardener. Statues, pots, and other pieces serve as metaphors for man, standing in the garden.

Gardens and art share the same territory of the soul, invoking possibilities beyond the material. Art enhances the hidden order of nature, and gardeners realize that careful placement in the garden can elevate even the most ordinary objects to the realm of art.

ABOVE: A small set of raised beds ascending like stairsteps adds dimension to the shade garden. This design by Penelope Hobhouse eschews the standard railroad tie or landscape timber for an intricately woven wattle fence.

OPPOSITE: Benches are a welcoming touch in any garden, offering respite from a busy world. These ceramic seats establish a modern motif on the patio. The cylinder introduces pattern and color and can function as a side table, while the crouching ceramic cat adds a bit of whimsy.

ABOVE LEFT: A Florentine urn brings a classical emphasis to the garden. By planting it with boxwood, you can avoid an empty look through the winter. The mossy, weathered appearance of the urn is accented by snow.

ABOVE RIGHT: Completely intriguing and somewhat exotic, this arrangement of shells, crab claws, and stones rising on driftwood stakes above a bed of cheery nasturtiums shows an irreverence and a sense of humor, as well as creative use of natural objects, in this seaside garden.

OPPOSITE: A curved, wooden garden bench lends a Victorian air to the garden; its unfinished wood provides a counterpoint to the bed of bright spring bulbs. It's easy to imagine women in flowing white gowns and men in formal wear strolling the grounds.

OPPOSITE: Tucked in among the foxgloves, this bench is a perfect place for sharing secrets—the splashing of water over a millstone adds a background of sound to mask the words.

BELOW: A birdbath is a must to make your garden come alive with the song of feathered visitors. The classical lines of this stone birdbath fit in perfectly with the well-trimmed hedges and carefully planned perennials.

ABOVE: A small, backyard water garden is integrated into the landscape with the help of garden ornaments. These stone frogs and fish enhance the aquatic theme.

BELOW: Glossy black stones contribute a mysterious, ancient look in this Japanese garden. Though inanimate, their look changes from day to day, turning flat and gray in the sunlight, and glistening darkly in the rain.

ABOVE: The rounded form of this pergola frames a magnificent urn, which draws visitors down the path. These elements harmonize beautifully with fragrant roses and wisteria to create a sense of order and balance.

ABOVE: The best garden ornaments reinforce a sense of place. There's no doubt that you're in the Southwest when you enter this garden: if the adobe wall and plant selection don't give it away, the carved sundial, wagon wheel, and Spanish-style statuary confirm the western locale.

ABOVE: This Japanese stone pool is a study in understatement. Nearly hidden by flowers and greenery, its clean lines and neutral colors celebrate simplicity.

RIGHT: We all want our landscapes to look established, no matter how recently they were planted. The worn stones and statue add a sense of history to this herb planting. If your property isn't already endowed with such weathered features, hunt for them at architectural salvage yards.

RIGHT: The moon, the stars, the sun, indeed all of nature play a vital role in the garden. A simple wall plaque reminds us that even the smallest planting is ruled by nature's forces.

BELOW: Brightly colored molas hang from clotheslines against a rustic fence, an arrangement reminiscent of a South American marketplace. The colors mirror the flowers below and help to add a festive, exotic air to the garden.

ABOVE: Cheerful spring bulbs are paired with a brightly painted chair for a color-drenched effect. The sunny yellow chair, bright blue door, and multicolored ceramic pot unify the small plantings, which can be somewhat jarring if they're the only spots of color in the landscape.

RIGHT: Sometimes a utilitarian piece in an eye-opening color is accent enough: these watering cans brighten the green and gray backdrop. They add a casual feeling as well, as though they were just set down between tasks.

ABOVE: A dark, damp corner of a shade garden is a perfect spot for a stone gargoyle to stand watch. His inscrutable face adds an eerie quality to his surroundings, a feeling that is only heightened by the abandoned homemade broom.

OPPOSITE: The garden becomes a magical place when imagination is allowed free reign. Here, hand-blown glass decanters filled with violet- and lilac-tinted water echo the bloom colors in this city garden. The color of the water can be changed to mirror the surrounding blooms.

ABOVE: A garden accent can be as large as a house—a greenhouse in this case. The lines and sharp angles of the structure, along with its startling, white color, anchor this garden, adding a bit of order to the jumble of plants.

OPPOSITE: Rules are often suspended in rooftop gardens. Furniture, such as this mosaic table, becomes a vital element of the design. And normally earthbound plants are tended in wall-hung pots; the containers thus become an integral part of the garden plan.

ABOVE: The wheel of thyme grinds exceedingly slowly in this garden! This visual pun serves as a perfect raised bed for a tiny herb garden; several varieties can be grown efficiently in a small space while kept separate by the spokes of the wheel.

LEFT: A garden path can be one of the most influential accents in the garden. It directs visitors toward areas of special beauty, and its arrangement and spacing subtly control the traveler's pace. Here, slices of log look right at home with the natural plantings.

OPPOSITE: Cast-iron benches, a favorite of nineteenth-century gardeners, bring quaint charm to outdoor spots. The lacy, scalloped back of this bench matches the frilly edges of the old-fashioned iris in the foreground. Both plant and accent are products of the Victorian age, making a stroll down the stone path a step back in time.

Chapter One

PRACTICAL ACCENTS

*O*ver the course of time every garden accumulates objects: benches, pots, birdhouses, fences, trellises, sheds. It's the rare garden that consists solely of plants.

In the working landscape, utility rules. Here, items are often chosen and placed according to practical considerations, with little or no thought to their decorative value. They either recede into the background or dominate a yard.

But even the most practical of accents can be artfully fused with the landscape. First, choose a style that harmonizes with the plants and your design. Older, classical pots and benches, for example, fit in with formal perennial beds and wide expanses of lawn. Modern or rustic chairs and trellises are better suited to an informal, natural planting.

Pay attention, too, to placement. Use these practical accents to draw attention to special areas of the landscape. Or set them out of the way, where they can blend into and complement groups of plants. Consider carefully the mood of the garden, and choose your accents accordingly.

OPPOSITE: Elevating a bench is an excellent way to give it prominence in the landscape. At the same time, you're creating a seating area with a spectacular view of the garden.

RIGHT: When vines are allowed to grow over a gazebo, its lines are softened and the structure blends into the garden seamlessly. This leafy bower provides a cool refuge from the summer heat.

LEFT: This bench is a crafty blend of simplicity and sophistication, with its geometric cutouts and its cleverly inset pots. The classic terra-cotta pots can be planted with various herbs and flowers throughout the year to make the most of the season.

OPPOSITE: A brightly colored, five-legged seat is undeniably the focal point in this garden spot. The low stone wall leading to a bridge is a perfect place to sit and enjoy the landscape.

RIGHT: The garden is a creation in color, and when garden accents are part of the equation, the results can be stunning. This vibrant combination of fuchsia, terra-cotta, and wavy lines of aqua would be difficult to achieve with plants alone.

OPPOSITE: The mosaic of blooms echoes the intricate pattern of tiles on this planter. Container gardening allows tremendous variety with little investment of time or space.

RIGHT: Behold a palace fit for visitors from the heavens. Elaborate pieces, like this Oriental-style birdhouse, are often best admired against a simple backdrop of greenery.

BELOW: An unexpected coupling of plant and pot makes a dramatic statement. While a flowering plant might be an obvious choice, the clean, simple lines of an agave plant draw attention without competing with the ornate urn.

ABOVE: An eternal, uncomplaining watchman, this scarecrow steadfastly guards an herb and vegetable garden. While he may allow the occasional bird to slip by, there's no doubt that he is largely responsible for the old-fashioned, farm-country feel of his surroundings.

OPPOSITE: Gardens come alive when birds call them home. A rustic, wooden bird feeder, attractive in its own right, lures these living, flying garden ornaments.

RIGHT: The silvery gray of weathered wood and the deep green of foliage are a natural combination in the garden. A birdhouse nestled among the sedums and potted herbs imparts the tranquillity found in miniature gardens.

BELOW: Something as prosaic as a row of mailboxes becomes a delightfully practical accent when splashed with bright colors and paired with equally colorful blooms.

ABOVE: Sometimes the most successful ornamentation derives from objects placed out of context. These antique coal oil lanterns, when placed in the garden, are seen in a new light. At the same time, they can serve a practical purpose, illuminating an evening picnic or a late-night stroll.

LEFT: This charming signpost is little more than a stenciled wooden stake, yet it successfully evokes the flavor of the English countryside. Garden signs like this and vegetable and herb markers are easy to make, serve to identify your plants, and add a cozy touch to your garden.

ABOVE: Some gardens are at their best when framed by a fence. This bright Japanese fence enhances the feeling of the spare plantings and the sleek sculpture.

OPPOSITE: A charming footbridge adds a goodly dose of color while uniting the garden by spanning a little stream.

RIGHT: A wrought-iron fence holds at bay the wild garden beyond. It encloses an area without seeming impenetrable, as witnessed by the wisteria threatening to climb over and through.

Chapter Two

FORMAL ACCENTS

*A*t some time or another, every gardener harbors dreams of grandeur. We envision our modest landscapes as kin to the great formal gardens of Europe, and we entertain the desire to invest some majesty in our own backyard.

Whether we're taken with the serious demeanor of a Renaissance parterre or the more lighthearted look of an Italian rococo garden, we all fantasize. In fact, many yards, with their rectangular shapes and broad expanses of lawn, are well-suited for a bit of classical treatment.

Formal accents can dictate the design of the garden itself, suggesting geometric patterns, straight lines, and long vistas with an ornament as the focal point. Or perhaps your garden is better suited to an Oriental simplicity with sparse plantings of simple combinations of plants and colors. Proceed with caution and with a unified sense of design, and your classical dreams can come true.

OPPOSITE: Appropriate placement, size, and tone coalesce to make this a highly successful example of classic garden ornament. The Egyptian-style statue sits in the middle of the path without obscuring the vista and the plants beyond. Its subdued color allows it to rest harmoniously in the landscape.

RIGHT: A Japanese lantern anchors a corner of a sedate landscape. Its rusty earthtones are mirrored by the rock at its base. When illuminated on a summer evening, it brings a soft luster to the garden.

ABOVE: The wealth of classical statuary in this tiny garden is almost tongue-in-cheek. The air of antiquity is emphasized by the overgrown weeds, the tangle of flowers in the planter, and the rough, tumble-down look of the stones; the spare green plant scheme doesn't include loud colors that could fight with the ornaments.

OPPOSITE: This sundial, nestled into a dense thicket of leaves, celebrates world exploration with its aged, stately ship perched atop a globe of metal bands.

ABOVE LEFT: Statues are usually placed on pedestals in the garden. By setting this bust low in the midst of a bulb bed, the gardener beautifully integrates the sculpture with the plants.

ABOVE RIGHT: Water is a desirable feature in classical gardens. The soothing sound and motion of water suggest serenity. The arching wall frames the entire arrangement.

OPPOSITE: The vertical line of this urn, set boldly atop a stone plinth, has a magnetic effect, pulling viewers toward it. Yet it is subtle enough in color, size, and shape that it doesn't vie with the planting. The tall, rather stern look of the planter tames the somewhat unruly phlox growing around it.

LEFT: An unusual, dramatic accent can transform a landscape. All eyes are drawn to this giant sunken chessboard. Most plantings would be overwhelmed by such large, imaginative garden art, but this expansive lawn extends the game board theme. The shrubs echo the playing pieces.

OPPOSITE: Mood is set by both placement and profile. Nestled against a stone wall, overgrown by ivy, and nearly obscured by centranthus, this statue creates a feeling of being absorbed by nature. The contemplative look on the face of the statue reinforces the impression.

BELOW: Exotic stone statues silently guard a wide set of stairs. The sense of mystery is enhanced by the manner in which the plants grow around them: it's as though you've stumbled into an ancient, abandoned palace garden.

ABOVE: Statues don't have to be classical in nature. This luminous blue bust juxtaposes a modern element with the primeval quality of a natural woodland garden.

OPPOSITE: With forethought and a strong sense of design, any area of the garden can serve as a site for a constructed accent. In this unusual arrangement, a trio of sculptures rises out of the pond on pedestals that recall tentacles, bridging the gap between man-made and organic forms.

RIGHT: A stone path brings order to a jubilant planting of roses and verbena. It leads, in classical fashion, to a weathered urn on a pedestal. This feature quietly beckons us forward and through the garden. The wattle fence at the end softens the feeling of enclosure.

ABOVE: A sundial takes us back to a simpler time, to an era when we weren't ruled by clocks and deadlines, and subliminally encourages us to stop and relax for a bit. The rough, uncut stone and primitive design of the piece reinforce the Edenic quality of the planting.

OPPOSITE: By its very form, art can infuse a setting with spirit. This exuberant sculpture adds a feeling of joie de vivre to a mass planting of sweet coltsfoot. It's easy to picture this wetland garden visited by sprites and spirits.

Chapter Three

CASUAL ACCENTS

*L*ike blank verse, an informal or modern garden at first seems easy to fashion because there are no rules to follow, no prescriptions to obey. Ironically, it is this absence of guidelines that can make planning the casual garden difficult to do well.

Anything goes in the contemporary garden: the invasion of plastic flamingos is proof of that. But not everything works. Even if the mood of your garden is light and whimsical, accents should be carefully chosen and artfully placed. The plants should always be given center stage, with ornaments taking a supporting, albeit important, role.

Consider the feeling you want your garden to convey. The range of accents you can find for a casual garden allows you to use folk art to create a cozy oasis or to incorporate kitschy pieces that amuse your visitors. This is the perfect opportunity to infuse your garden with your own personality, whether it be warm and earthy or playfully outrageous.

OPPOSITE: Gardens provide a link to the past, to a time when life was less complicated. Here, an antique water pump helps build the illusion of stepping back in time. The plantings around it are kept simple to further that feeling.

RIGHT: Formal topiary in pots contrasts with a rough, wooden chair that looks not far removed from the tree that supplied the material. The dark form of a globular vase adds a modern touch and repeats the undulating lines of the sun mosaic.

ABOVE: When choosing ornaments for the garden, select those that preserve a sense of the region. Formal garden art would seem out of place in this Southwestern xeriscape planting. But a mosaic dais, paired with a simple birdhouse, captures the simple, geometric patterns of Native American art.

OPPOSITE: Indoors, the function of a birdcage sometimes overrides its graceful form. But outdoors, adorning a mottled, vermilion wall, this rainbow-colored aviary, grounded by the potted geraniums below, completes a perfect garden picture.

RIGHT: A patio or balcony railing transcends the functional with the aid of a few fanciful elements. At the same time, it's an ideal location to hang flowering plants like these geraniums.

ABOVE: The sweeping, almost musical form of a sundial soars from a bed of herbs in a modern city garden. Nearby, a redwood bench with an unusual, sunrise-shaped back offers a place to sit and watch the passage of time.

LEFT: The spare form of a metal sundial mellows when morning glories are encouraged to creep in and contribute their brilliant color to the scene.

OPPOSITE: Often, unused structures on a property can be turned to advantage rather than torn down. Here, an old stone well has been transformed into a rising rock garden with a planting of sedums and other rock garden plants. The embellished wrought-iron pail support arching over the well supplies additional architectural interest.

ABOVE: Folk art, too, makes a welcome accent in a casual setting. This primitive carved and painted statue adds a Caribbean feeling to the garden. The bright beads link the piece to the dazzling colors of the surrounding plantings.

OPPOSITE: Woven vines make fine weatherproof material for garden accents. They can be fashioned into any number of imaginative shapes and forms, such as these woven wood geese.

ABOVE: Kitchen gardens of the eighteenth century inspired this little plot, where a bee skep on a pedestal holds a place of honor. These hives, made of twisted straw, attract bees to pollinate plants and provide a source of honey. Nowadays, they are often purely ornamental, lending a traditional, homey touch to any garden.

LEFT: A rustic gazebo, reminiscent of a crude hayrack, effectively punctuates this wetland space without disrupting the wild feel. Built exclusively of natural materials, it looks almost like a nest for humans.

OPPOSITE: Even meadows and wildflower gardens can be improved by an accent. This gardener brings focus and a sense of history to the site by placing a traditional Southwestern horno oven in the midst of black-eyed Susans, sunflowers, daisies, and other blooms. The shape and color of the clay oven tie the entire landscape to the bluffs in the distance.

ABOVE LEFT: At their best, garden accents seduce visitors into viewing more than the scene immediately before them: rather than competing with the garden itself, effective ornaments offer encouragement to take in the entire sweep of the plantings. Though the bright red geraniums in the foreground may attract first attention, the bleached skull hanging from the adobe wall draws the eye to the back of the garden to automatically survey all the beds in between.

ABOVE RIGHT: Some of the most effective ornaments are the most simple. These shiny river stones in a small stream add a sense of serenity. Their shapes and texture create a transition between the running water and the upright plants. The tiny stone frogs bring the arrangement to life.

OPPOSITE: With the adobe walls and bricks carrying the feel of the desert into this garden room, the deadwood planter appears natural and completely in scale. It takes only a few common petunias to turn an old log into a charming garden accent.

ABOVE: The fresh-looking color scheme of luminous white flowers and green leaves and pots has been carried over to the antique watering can. The sizable dent somehow adds to the charm, convincing us that the can has been well used and the potted garden has been well tended.

LEFT: Ivy drifts across the face of a plaster plaque, creating the illusion of clouds moving to cover the sun. Well-placed garden ornaments not only add a decorative element, they can also bring a new dimension to the plants.

OPPOSITE: Playfulness grows in this garden. An elaborate fountain constructed of shells offers a strong clue to this gardener's disposition. The visual rhyme of shells and water, along with the whimsical mask of Hermes, leaves no doubt that this person enjoys the garden.

Chapter Four

ACCENTS IN THE LANDSCAPE

*I*nfatuation with ornaments should not be allowed to grow into blind love. Remember that accents are intended to highlight the plantings, not upstage them.

Always keep the mood of your garden in mind when choosing ornaments, and plan the type of ornament according to the garden style. Classical pieces will always enhance a formal garden, while modern or folk art is more appropriate for a casual garden.

Beyond that advice, there are a few guidelines to follow:

• Be aware of scale. Ornaments should not overpower a small planting or recede to the point of oblivion in a large one.

• Consider sight lines and perspective. Choose accents with strong vertical elements for open expanses of lawn; cluster smaller objects in corners of plantings.

• Note the way light and shadow play across your garden. Place large objects where rays of sunlight will spotlight them during certain periods of the day. Or nestle small objects in shady nooks. Use vines, trees, and plants with plentiful foliage as backdrops for statues or brightly colored ornaments.

• Look for natural curves or upright habits in plants and mirror them with arching or vertical accents.

• Keep an eye out for the best vantage points for accents. Place ornaments so that they can be enjoyed from patios, porches, walkways, or windows.

Finally, have fun accenting your landscape, and don't be afraid to take a chance by violating the rules.

OPPOSITE: A stone urn overflowing with marguerites, helichrysum, and nicotiana immediately attracts attention: the delicate flowering plants are lifted to a place of honor. If planted in the ground, they might have been overlooked or overpowered by other plants.

ABOVE: Sometimes there's impact in numbers. Found objects often make the greatest impression when they're grouped together. The combination of textures, materials, shapes, and colors makes this an interesting corner of a wild landscape.

ABOVE: A thoughtful garden design matches accents with plants and with the overall milieu of the garden. This worn and weathered chair would look unkempt on a lawn, but it seems perfectly at home tucked beneath a similarly weathered picket fence covered with rambling, old-fashioned roses.

LEFT: Design and form can provide important cues for good placement of accents. The rustic material, simple design, and subdued colors of this handmade chair coordinate perfectly with the farmlike setting.

OPPOSITE: A healthy dose of imagination can result in accents that quite literally become part of the garden. Here, simple kitchen chairs take on a fairy tale aspect when planted with moss and wrapped in twisting vines. They ensure that this spot of the garden will continue to entertain even through the winter months.

ABOVE: The coppery sheen of the shallow pool's bottom sets off the green of the surrounding herbs, while the border of verdigris tiles extends the leafy theme. The water enhances the beauty of the plants by reflecting their image in its surface.

RIGHT: A simple stone basin makes a fine garden accent all through the year. But placed beneath a maple, it is bound to catch the leaves from above, making it come alive with red and gold in the autumn.

OPPOSITE: A unique arrangement of turf and stone in a checkerboard design fits best in the corner of a wide expanse of lawn. The hulking shrubs serve as living metaphors for chess pieces.

RIGHT: Diminutive, churchlike birdhouses, complete with steeples, are a welcome surprise when removed from their normal, airy location and placed near the ground amid a grouping of terra-cotta pots. They emphasize the flowering plants by bringing a new focus to the scene.

OPPOSITE: An old stone springhouse has been incorporated into this picturesque water garden. Reminiscent of an ancient grotto, it provides a natural transition from the bog planting to the dry-land plants surrounding it. Flowers planted atop the structure help to integrate it into the landscape.

BELOW: An unmowed meadow scattered with spikes of foxglove looks almost like an accidental planting. Carefully overturn some textured urns in a variety of earthy hues, and the entire scene comes together with the mystery of an ancient tableau.

ABOVE: Some ornaments work best when they are made to mimic nature. These whimsical rabbits peer out from foliage to delight passing children and other nature lovers.

OPPOSITE: The style and color of an accent should be carefully selected to fit the surrounding garden. This artful, monochromatic piece complements the planting with its simplicity of form. The green foliage, in turn, allows the statue its place in the sun.

INDEX

PHOTO CREDITS